for keith
at Snape

Bridge Pamphlet
No.3

with best wishes

Peter

Nov 2015

X

THE NIGHT IS YOUNG

Peter Sansom has made 'a sort of living' from poetry for over twenty years. His Carcanet books are 'witty, realistic and imaginative' – *Observer*, winning awards and a loyal readership, while his *Writing Poems*, Bloodaxe 1994, is still said to change writing lives.

Peter has been Fellow in Poetry at both Leeds and Manchester Universities, and company poet for M&S and the Prudential. He is a director with Ann Sansom of The Poetry Business in Sheffield, where they edit *The North* magazine and Smith/Doorstop Books.

PETER SANSOM

THE NIGHT IS YOUNG

THE RIALTO

ACKNOWLEDGEMENTS

Many thanks to the editors of the following, where several of these poems first appeared: *The Manchester Review, Poetry Review, Smiths Knoll* and *Stand*.

The warmest of thanks also to John McAuliffe and Ian McGuire of the Centre for New Writing at the University of Manchester, where most of this collection was happily unwritten and written again.

BRIDGE PAMPHLETS

This is the third in a series of *The Rialto* pamphlets designed to cross the gap between magazine and book publication for new writers or, for established writers, that between collections..

First published in 2009 by
The Rialto
PO Box 309 Aylsham Norwich
England NR11 6LN
www.therialto.co.uk

ISBN 9780955127342
The publisher acknowledges financial assistance from
the Arts Council of England, East.

The Rialto is a Registered Charity No. 297553
Typeset in Berling 10 on 12.5pt
Design by Starfish, Norwich.
Printed by Micropress Limited.
Cover Photograph, Max Westby.

For Ann and for everyone here

CONTENTS

POP BOTTLE

Better than pop, in fact, the water swigged
from the bottle we took turns to carry
through the sweltering summer down the gardens
(fields and allotments), the lane ('unadopted')
of no-puddles in the pot-holes and mother-die
white we pushed through head high at the stile.
It's still heavy that glass, dimpled at the neck
like frost later, a world on the window
when you pulled back the curtains for school,
still dark behind it, black in fact, despite the snow.

RIVER

I love to paddle back
forty years, more, in the hurry-shallows
among the pebbles,
beyond the half-in
half-out stepping stones,
where it goes on, plural, one,
from cloud on mountain to here
from living spring and stream sent
underground to here, and further,
socks in pockets
shoes in hands
like a tightrope, trousers rolled
a boy for the sticklebacks
a stopped shadow, eddies
all glooble and gloop,
paper boat
paper boat to the weir.

STEP-LADDER

Built and bought to wallpaper with
and stand four-square sturdy while I change
a bulb or fit some blinds, it mostly leans
on hind legs into bookshelves in this high room,
Hamson, Hanff, and the whole gamut of Hardy,
Desperate Remedies to *Jude the Obscure*.
Every so often I climb among the summer
I spent in Wessex and blow the dust
off a page or two of then, plugged in to Santana
and him at midnight bowing it higher.
I stood there an hour the other day lost
at the ceiling on Egdon Heath,
the boy I was, while my tea went cold;
and though this morning I'm only here
to start again on the kitchen, who could resist
those four treads up to step back in time
with the reddleman and Eustacia Vye?

AUTUMN TERM

You couldn't call it grief, but it's something
to not hug, just smile by the stairs to Y6,
and retrace my steps across the hopscotch.
I don't stop to not see her in Miss Duke's
magic cave of a room, whose tables and chairs
made a giant of me on open-door Thursdays,
when we snuggled together in picturebooks
more colourful than life can stay. No, I walk on.
But even so, and though it's coming on to rain,
I detour through the park, to maunder down days
when the tall-tall slide and climbing frame
were terrifying though she mustn't know;
and find myself beneath the leaky umbrella
of an oak, late for work, while the brilliant leaves
let go and fall slowly like stones through water,
so lovely, despite me, I should laugh
at myself, the picture of misery; but I don't.

KEYMARKETS

Day-in day-out without natural light the winter
they rationed butter and eggs (strikes;
the three day week) – working for peanuts but even so,
despite the aisle on aisle of facing tins and jars
and the late hours in the warehouse, it was just
the best of times. One night we climbed
the stacked cases me and my best mate to sit
above the shift with cans of continental lager
high among the iron rafters. There was a party
at a girl's and Lindisfarne's *Nicely Out Of Tune*
to take to it – and, though years later they pumped
my stomach because of her, what matters is
nobody missed us or happened to look up
between clocking-in and our stint last thing
horsing with the cardboard bailer. Canada,
he lives now, and I of course live here,
though in many ways we're still up there. Cheers.

'I USED TO FAINT'

I used to faint at the sight of blood.
That cauldron of early teens, even the idea
of blood and the thought of fainting
brought the self-conscious beating
in my ears, gripping my throat,
so that I almost literally died
of embarrassment. Being grown up
was an age away and was not waking
but coming a long way back
to their faces – every time, even at home,
with the same empty-headed 'Where am I?'
that they couldn't help smiling at.
It surprised me last week, a test
for the diabetes that killed my brother,
to pass out. It was just as far
and humiliating to be no age at all, my body
knowing better than me its own mind,
and it was just as bewildering
where I came back to.

PETAR K., 1957-2007

Despite misreading a bend and coming to
in a field you thought was death but was only
your helmet jammed over your eyes, and laughing
that laugh of yours despite the pain, you were soon
out again testing the endless flat A-roads of Lincolnshire.
I think that's how it always was, and so it's him, not you,
I feel for, who turned unaccountably in front
of your sixty miles an hour. And what I want to say
from my life, my heated seats Volvo,
I want to say it's too long now, and though it's great
you liked your funeral, packed out the doors, and bringing
the sun in, *Always Look On The Bright Side Of Life*,
listen Petar, isn't it time you came back? The roads
are still there with their danger right across the fens if you like,
all those roads a sea dried between islands forever
all that sea really road after road between spires,
change down for the level crossing, the patient
speed-limit in and out of a sleepy village, then go,
open her up, letting all our schoolboy years fall behind.

BEST FRIEND

It's for you, you said
in the advert voice, but
when I pressed it to my ear
it was Donny Osmond,
Puppy Love. Dial-a-disc,
in the 70s, it didn't last.
I knew why you did it.
I was sixteen and it
wasn't puppy love – though
when she said drop dead
you had the wit to tell me
she was a dog.

IN THE CAIRNGORMS

The highest mainline railway
in Britain, and just as I say it
                    we rock to a stop;
            the coffee ripples in your cup.

Scots pine and silver birch bend
            to other days' winds;
somewhere soon
            is snow at Aviemore
but this window is grey-green

splashed with bright cagoules
                        in the rain.
Dad with the map
                points to a hill
            but mum and the kids
are looking at us.

They wave and we
            wave back
                    as we pull away.

IN INVERNESS-SHIRE

Surprising, this second spring of harebell
and day-old lambs we saw last month. Likewise
new-leaf oak and aspen, and, close-to, brilliant gorse
that only yards away is dimmed, like home.
The days start so early here that this morning
I set off walking an hour or two the passing-place roads
that go dead straight then plunge where they like, rising
with the curve of acre on acre of wind-struck trees.
Now and then farmsteads, each with its caravan
and mailbox on the road, but still no people –
and there's no-one even in my head, even family,
till here for some reason is the child
whose fourth birthday was international news,
who just a month ago was safe, and whose parents
can't go back to save her and themselves.
It's a kind of trespass, I know, thinking this,
because I can walk on and unthink it, which I do,
among the identical miles of trees, the mountains seen now
from a bend in the road, their lunar tracks and tarns,
the bivouacs of bright surviving snow.

MOON

We stayed up late in the old house
and when we somehow turned to talking
about the moon landing
more than a decade before you were born
we stood in the doorway
to look at it
yellow as sand through trees
by the spire of St Aidan's.
Impossible to believe
that people stood there
and looked back.
Impossible to believe,
actually, how soon you've grown.
To you, naturally,
even a dozen years
before you were born
is ancient history,
though to me a moon landing
still seems like the future.

CROFT JUNIORS

is a playground I stand looking out at, forty years;
empty tarmac, the long minutes before morning break.
A cat crosses it. Then the caretaker, nameless now;
and Mr Shooter, the Head, still with a rack of canes –
likewise our teacher, Mr Alsop, would use the side of a ruler,
no nonsense in his class. I can taste the texture
of penny wafers, and open my orange RE book at Moses;
toy-size bottles of milk are warming by a radiator,
and I can still smell the toilets (a wall outside to compete on),
still hear us dancing in pumps to a Dansette in the hall.
I remember match-day, longing for the bell,
the boxes of kit, one with 'sox' on it, and the jerseys,
bright yellow cotton, white button collars, though mine
was moss green. I remember diving and Mr Shooter
shouting from the touchline, even after all this time
no idea who I am, 'Well saved, goalkeeper.'

MY BROTHER'S VESPA

Red, scarlet even, it meant fun
and something more, stylish, Italian
on a stand, in the yard. The chrome
shone, the handlegrips revved
to Cleethorpes in my head, my hair
a quiff I wanted to dye black, for him
not Elvis – he was Elvis. When he
climbed a ladder to the moon
on the roof for my ball he was a hero
like the pictures he took me to.
He could live forever.
He did. First we live
then we remember.

A STRAW HAT

On a hook by the window, with another
that the youngest grew out of. Here it is
knocked off by the wave I didn't see,
laughing, a mouth full of sea. But yours
where did it go, last-minute-anywhere-hot hat,
'hello' and 'thank you' all we could say
by the pool, or a dusty train into the mountains. Gone,
while this persists, a real dad's hat,
under the tree he never had, the books
he never read, unravelling at the edge of shade, sweat
in the salt-stained band. I tip it back. Shoot me
if I wear it into town or a steady walk
to the pub. It bobs like a cork in the past
and present world, I take it off to you
love of my life, light of my life, willing
to walk with me even in a hat like this.

STATION BUFFET

Quicker to say where you shouldn't change
at Crewe for. Mid-week mid-journey
with the local paper and a mug of tea
by a steamed-up window, this cosy church
of being nowhere much
suits me. You could date it
by the tinfoil ashtrays and set your watch
by the radio. The walls are a gallery
of smoothies and pies. The fruit machine
is a bandit. And now it's raining, lovely.
The tannoy is a gazetteer, and I listen
to pick out my train, sometimes I read
the timetable or remember the canal at dusk,
the mist that travels with it standing still. Stay here
long enough and everyone you know
will pass through. I puzzled at a story
some time before I saw the headline
was 'scenes' not 'scones'. You'd have laughed.

DECREPIT

It's like I've hiked all night
some mornings, bending
for the milk, grunting
like a first serve (the nearest
I get these days to sport).

I met a teacher yesterday
with the Antarctic Survey.
He told me like a slide-show about it:
the blank screen of snow
the black screen of the tent
when they heard someone walking,
and struggled out to shine
their torches in the polar dark
and find nothing –
except footprints.

Most of their time at base
was playing darts on the radio
with the Norwegians:
they'd throw in one hut
and get the Norwegian score
from another a mile away.

I never think of my soul
but last night there was me
on the oche of the timeless ice
having just stepped out the house
for a breather at minus thirty.

And this morning don't I
know about it, like an old man
setting off as far as the fridge, the kettle,
as far as the toaster, leaving the grunt
of a footprint everywhere I go.

THE NIGHT IS YOUNG

I have drunk
a highland malt that took my head off
to show willing at two in the morning,
the odd glass of red with a meal for my heart
and a pint of shandy at the quiz,
but not
let my hair down sick as a dog
hair of the dog, not *drunk* drunk,
not for years, and even then, hormones
everywhere, never lost it completely
brought back a curry in a taxi
on a girlfriend, not said
what I didn't know I meant *it was*
the drink talking
not Friday night drunk or office party
drunk in charge of a photocopier
let's have some fun
as Jane Austen said
on this reckless planet.

God help me to get to this age
and never *what a great night that was*
if only I could remember it
completely and utterly
drunk? Me? Not ever,
not yet.

SHALESMOOR, SHEFFIELD

Turning off eventually out of a jam,
I park up down the side street of another country –
Furnace Hill and Foundry Court, and Snow Lane in August,
all of it derelict to the point of grass on roofs
and rosebay willowherb gawping from what's left
of windows on this unguided walk. I look twice
at two girls with pints and a dog in front of no pub –
only Cook's (Bearings) Ltd (To Let) – and walk through
their back and forth 'He never was' 'he was' 'he never',
so oblivious they might be ghosts, or I might.
The shell of The Princess Works of Stavely Brass Co
dwarfs the prefab of Newland UPVC; then,
cresting Scotland Street, I come out at West Bar's
state of the art cranes, hi-rise closing in
like combines flushing out the last wildlife
and razing the rare botany of die-cast and smeltings
down the pig-iron valley of yesteryear. I turn.
Yanks once touted the world's thinnest filament
to a firm round here, only to get it back
bored along its length. I like remembering that.
For answer, a carrier bag tumbleweeds past, startling me
and the girls and their dog no longer there.

MILLHOUSES PARK

Meanwhile, a toy boat
bobbed out on the pond, sailboat
among the remote
controlled. Oh, I listened down
to that scale, waves it braved
barely ripples. The crew
were at my side, the boom swung
across to duck under; the spray
was an adventure.

A pond in a park is childhood,
the far bank a lifetime away,
unbelievable. Look at the rain
marking the surface, look at the time.

INSTEAD OF GOING TO WORK

Instead of going to work I read a book.
I wasn't ill or particularly tired, there was
nothing at work I wanted to avoid, it wasn't
the sort of book you stay off work to read;
but even so I didn't go to work. Instead
I mowed the lawn, as if that was work, too damp
between drizzle, then sat with a cup of tea
and went on with the sort of book you put down
and never finish. I did the kitchen window,
as if that was work, then opened some soup
for lunch with the radio I didn't listen to,
and thought of a drive or a walk, the museum,
but instead I ironed a shirt and pottered round
on the piano, as if that was work, and had
the house to myself, talking to the cat and listening
to the rain, a real downpour, and tried not to feel
I should be doing more with the day
than the nothing I did instead of going to work.

MY TOWN

I don't bother trying to find it, it's not there,
a 60s precinct with Keymarkets and Syd Booths Records,
a dozen bakers diabetes fat determined women
wiry mining-stock men (though my family
were hosiery and Metal Box), and windy market awnings
that tipped rain on you. For passport
a squeaky seventies library, glass and spiral steps
and a girl like my wife crossing the bus station
biting into a green apple, all style, grace, so that
I lived through her by the window of 821
with Milton and Robert Frost; the smell of polish;
just the idea of books (I could barely read,
always getting myself in the way); and *Harvest*,
the spyglass guest at the feast. But colourless I think
and the accent ugly. So why is it that miles from, years from
that town, hearing it I lie down in its warmth
somewhere off Portland Square, by the Kings Bingo mum
comes out of with her tartan wheelie-bag,
I lie there as if fallen a long way: drawn round
with chalk or magic marker maybe, another
piece of evidence essentially.
How would I know? Why should I care?
The Zombies sang that then
and they're still singing it.